MAY   2012

NOTE TO PARENTS

Welcome to Kingfisher Readers! This program is designed to help young readers build skills, confidence, and a love of reading as they explore their favorite topics.

These tips can help you get more from the experience of reading books together. But remember, the most important thing is to make reading fun!

Tips to Warm Up Before Reading

- Look through the book with your child. Ask them what they notice about the pictures.
- Wonder aloud together. Ask questions and make predictions. What will this book be about? What are some words we could expect to find on these pages?

While Reading

- Take turns or read together until your child takes over.
- Point to the words as you say them.
- When your child gets stuck on a word, ask if the picture could help. Then think about the first letter too.
- Accept and praise your child's contributions.

After Reading

- Look back at the things your child found interesting. Encourage connections to other things you both know.
- Draw pictures or make models to explore these ideas.
- Read the book again soon, to build fluency.

With five distinct levels and a wealth of appealing topics, the Kingfisher Readers series provides children with an exciting way to learn to read and wonder about the world around them. Enjoy!

Ellie Costa, M.S. Ed.
Literacy Specialist, Bank Street School for Children, New York

KINGFISHER READERS

level 2

Your Body

Brenda Stones and Thea Feldman

KINGFISHER
NEW YORK

KINGFISHER
LONDON & NEW YORK

Copyright © Kingfisher 2012
Published in the United States by Kingfisher,
175 Fifth Ave., New York, NY 10010
Kingfisher is an imprint of Macmillan Children's Books, London.
All rights reserved.

Distributed in the U.S. and Canada by Macmillan,
175 Fifth Ave., New York, NY 10010

Library of Congress Cataloging-in-Publication data
has been applied for.

Series editor: Thea Feldman
Literacy consultant: Ellie Costa, Bank St. College, New York
Commissioned photography by Howard Davies

ISBN: 978-0-7534-6756-5 (HB)
ISBN: 978-0-7534-6757-2 (PB)

Kingfisher books are available for special promotions
and premiums. For details contact: Special Markets
Department, Macmillan, 175 Fifth Ave., New York, NY 10010.

For more information, please visit
www.kingfisherbooks.com

Printed in China
9 8 7 6 5 4 3 2 1
1TR/0811/WKT/UNTD/105MA

Picture credits
The Publisher would like to thank the following for permission to reproduce their material.
Every care has been taken to trace copyright holders. However, if there have been unintentional
omissions or failure to trace copyright holders, we apologize and will, if informed, endeavor
to make corrections in any future edition.
Top = t; Bottom = b; Center = c; Left = l; Right = r
Cover Howard Davies; Pages 9t Shutterstock/Greenland; 9b Shutterstock/Andreas Gradin;
16b Shutterstock/Sebastian Kaulitzki; 17t Shutterstock/xjbxjhxm123; 19b Shutterstock/X.D. Luo;
25t Photofusion/Brian Mitchell; 25b Photofusion/Paula Solloway; 28t Shutterstock/Ramona Helm;
28–29 Shutterstock/Rob Marmion; 29t Shutterstock/Anyka; 31b Shutterstock/Rob Marmion; all other
photographs are by Howard Davies.

With special thanks to the following children for taking part in this book:
Jamie Andrews, Finley Chesson, Joe Chesson, Freya Cook, Joe Davies, Joe Dixon Bowley,
Ayobami James, Lena Hannigan, Sophia Ritchie, and Libbi Walsh.

Contents

Take a good look!

Look at you and your friends.

You can see hands, arms, feet, legs, eyes, and ears.

You can see the outside of the body!

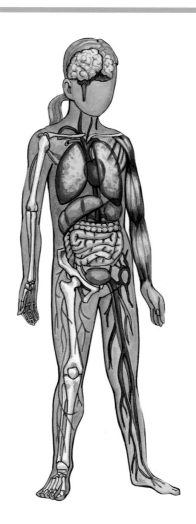

Here is what
the inside of the
body looks like.

Hands and arms

You do many things with
your hands and arms.

You throw and catch balls.

You push and pull things too.

You hold things in your hands.

You write and draw.

You brush your
teeth too!

Are you right-handed or
left-handed?

Feet and legs

Run, run, run!

You run with your feet and legs.

You walk, jump, and bend down too.

You can climb
with your feet
and legs.

Or you can kick
a ball.

You can stand
still too.

9

Eyes

You see with
your eyes.

Eyes can be
blue or brown.

They can be
green or gray too.

What color are
your eyes?

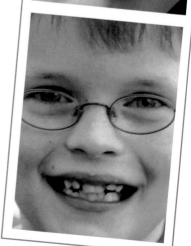

Ears

You hear with
your ears.

You can hear your
friend tell you a secret.

And you can hear music too.

What do you hear right now?

Nose

Sniff, sniff!

You smell things like flowers with your nose.

You breathe through your nose too.

Mouth

You eat and talk with your mouth.

You taste food with your tongue.

You chew food with your teeth.

Your tongue and teeth are inside your mouth.

Skin

You can feel things with your skin.

You can feel a kitten's whisker.

You can feel the sun too.

You have skin all over the outside of your body.

Hair

Hair can be short or long, straight or curly.

Hair can be blond or brown, red or black.

Hair helps keep you warm.

Bones

Inside your body you have 206 bones.

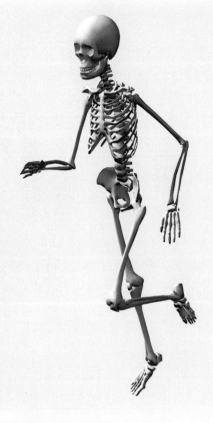

Bones are hard and they hold your body together.

They make up your **skeleton**.

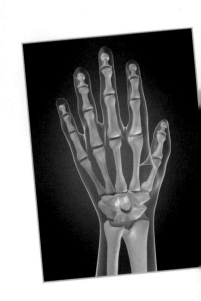

Half of your bones are tiny ones in your hands and feet.

Muscles

You have **muscles** inside your body too.

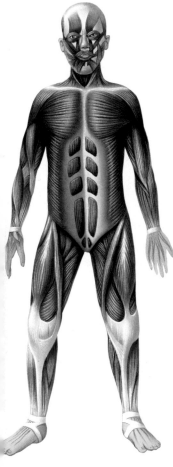

Muscles cover your bones.

They move your hands, arms, feet, legs, and much more.

You have 650 muscles!

Brain

You learn and think with your brain.

Your brain also sends messages to other parts of your body.

And it gets messages back too!

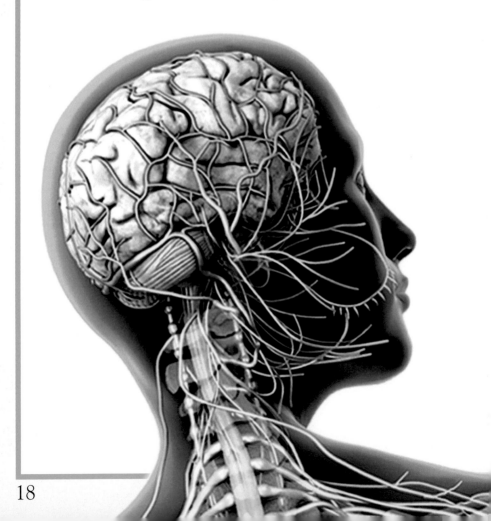

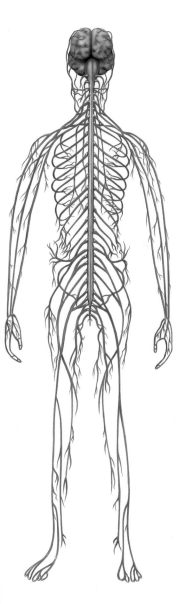

Nerves

Messages go through your **nerves**.

Nerves are like thin wires inside your body.

Your brain can tell your muscles to move.

It can tell you to take your hand away from something sharp.

Lungs

Take a deep breath.

You breathe with your lungs.

Fresh air goes from your nose
or mouth to
your lungs.

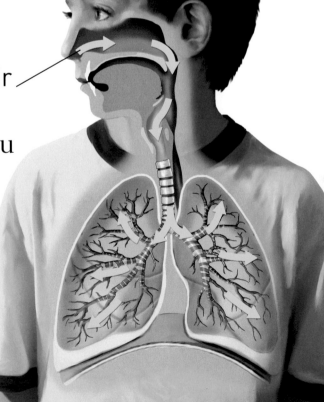

Air

When you
breathe
out, you
get rid
of old
air.

Blood

Your heart pumps blood around your body.

The blood moves through tubes.

A tube can be a **vein** or an **artery**.

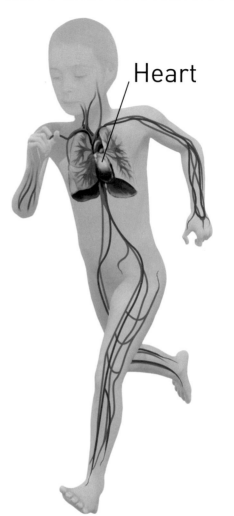

Heart

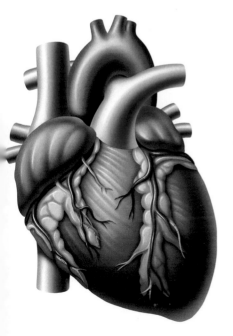

A vein carries blood to the heart.

An artery carries blood away from the heart.

Follow the food!

What did you have for breakfast today?

The food you chew gets small enough to swallow.

It goes to your stomach and gets even smaller.

Food goes from your stomach to your intestines.

You have a small intestine.

It sends the good parts of the food to the rest of your body.

You have a large intestine too.

It gets rid of the waste that is left.

Stomach

Small intestine

Large intestine

One of a kind!

No two people are the same.

Every person is one
of a kind.

Some people cannot walk.

They use wheelchairs to get where they need to go.

Some people cannot hear.

They use sign language to talk to other people.

Taking care of your body

Exercise can help you stay healthy.

Do you like to ride a bicycle?

A good night's sleep is important too.

So is eating good things like fruits and vegetables.

Remember to wash your hands before you eat!

Get well soon!

Everyone gets sick sometimes.

Achoo!

Have you ever had a cold or the flu?

Sometimes you need to see the doctor.

She can give you medicine to make you feel better.

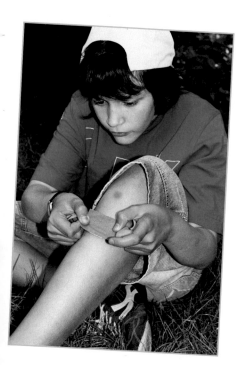

Have you ever needed a bandage?

A bandage covers a cut.

It keeps the cut clean.

This helps you get better.

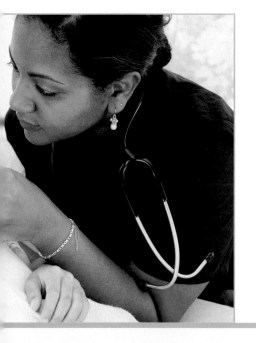

When you don't feel well, you need to rest.

That will help you get well soon!

You are growing!

Kids grow and change a lot.

Have you grown since last year?

Your hair probably has.

If you do not cut your hair,
it will grow 5 inches
(12 centimeters)
a year!

You are learning!

Every year you learn new things.

Your brain grows bigger too!

Did you learn new things in this book?

Glossary

artery a tube inside the body that carries blood away from the heart to other parts of the body

muscles the parts of the body that move the bones in the body

nerves thin wire-like parts inside the body that carry messages

skeleton all the bones in your body, which hold your body together

vein a tube inside the body that carries blood to the heart from other parts of the body

 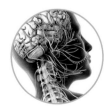 

If you have enjoyed reading this book, look out for more in the Kingfisher Readers series!

KINGFISHER READERS: LEVEL 1

Baby Animals
Butterflies
Colorful Coral Reefs
Jobs People Do
Snakes Alive!
Trains

KINGFISHER READERS: LEVEL 2

What Animals Eat
Your Body

KINGFISHER READERS: LEVEL 3

Dinosaur World
Volcanoes

KINGFISHER READERS: LEVEL 4

Pirates
Weather

KINGFISHER READERS: LEVEL 5

Ancient Egyptians
Rainforests

For a full list of Kingfisher Readers books, plus guidance for teachers and parents and activities and fun stuff for kids, go to the Kingfisher Readers website: **www.kingfisherreaders.com**